BLACK WIDOWS

BLACK WIDOWS

PETER MURRAY

THE CHILD'S WORLD

PHOTO RESEARCH
Charles Rotter/Gary Lopez Productions

PHOTO CREDITS
James H. Robinson: front cover,
back cover, 6, 14, 17, 18, 21, 24, 27, 28
Robert and Linda Mitchell: 2, 10
Joe McDonald: 9
Dr. Edward Ross: 13, 23
Leonard Lee Rue III: 31

Distributed to schools and libraries in the United States by
ENCYCLOPAEDIA BRITANNICA EDUCATIONAL CORP.
310 South Michigan Avenue
Chicago, Illinois 60604

Library of Congress Cataloging-in-Publication Data
Murray, Peter, 1952 Sept. 29–
Black Widows / by Peter Murray.
p.   cm.
Summary: Introduces the physical characteristics and
behavior of the black widow spider.
ISBN 0-89565-845-3
1. Black widow spider--Juvenile literature.
[1. Black widow spider. 2. Spiders.]   I. Title.
QL458.42.T54M87   1992   92-3332
595.4'4--dc20   CIP
                                                 AC

For Brittany

A tangled web of fine silk. You might find one in a dark corner of an old building, or under your front steps, or even somewhere inside your house. You might find one under a bench, or behind a trunk in the attic. It might be only a few inches across, or several feet. It won't look like the neat, orderly spider webs you see in books. The strands of this web seem to go every which way. Look closely, and you will probably find a spider. If the spider is black and shiny, be careful! You may have discovered the home of a deadly black widow.

Most spiders are not dangerous to humans. Their fangs are too small, and their venom is too weak to hurt us. Even the giant tarantula, which can grow up to ten inches across, is harmless. In North America there is only one spider that can seriously harm a human being—the female black widow! This small spider has venom so powerful that its bite can make a person very sick. People who are bitten usually recover, but some have died from the bite of the black widow!

Black widows live in every state except Alaska. In some southern states they are one of the most common spiders. They often hide their tangled webs in dark corners. Unless you are looking for them, you might never know they are there.

If you find the web of a black widow, the spider will probably be hiding at the back. The black widow is shy, and you are too big for it to eat, so it wants nothing to do with you. But don't disturb its web! The black widow does not like trespassers.

Black widows are not insects. Like all spiders, they belong to a group of animals called *arachnids*. They have eight legs, eight eyes, and a body that is divided into two parts. The front part of a spider's body is called the *cephalothorax*. It contains the brain, eyes, mouth, stomach, feelers, poison glands, and fangs. The back part of a spider is called the *abdomen*. It contains the heart, lungs, silk glands, and spinnerets.

Black widows eat insects. The spider waits for a fly or some other insect to get caught in its sticky web. When the black widow feels the vibrations of a captured insect, it runs out and throws a layer of silk over the struggling victim. If the insect continues to struggle, the black widow bites it and injects a dose of venom. After sucking the insect dry, the black widow cuts it loose from its web, and the dead husk falls to the ground.

Male and female black widows are very different. The female black widow spider has a shiny black body about the size of a large pea. One sure way to identify the female is to look for a reddish orange hourglass-shaped spot on its belly.

The female black widow usually spends her entire life in one place. She lives about a year. If you look under the web of a full-grown female, you will find the ground littered with the husks of dead insects. One black widow spider ate 255 flies, two crickets, and a caterpillar.

The male black widow is only about half the size of the female. It has red or white stripes on its back. Male black widows have weak venom and are harmless to humans.

The male black widow lives for only a few months. As soon as he is full grown, he leaves his web in search of a mate. When he finds the web of a female black widow, he approaches very, very carefully. The male touches the female's web and makes it vibrate. If the female returns the vibrations, it means she is ready to mate. If the female is not ready to mate, she might eat the male for lunch!

If he isn't chased away, the male moves onto the web and uses his long legs to tap and stroke the female. After they mate, the male quickly leaves the web. If he is not quick enough, he might become his mate's next meal. That is why these spiders are called black widows. Sometimes the male brings the female an insect wrapped in silk. If the female accepts the gift, she will not be so hungry, and she may let him stay in her web for a few days.

After mating, the female black widow makes a silk pouch called an *egg sac*. The sac is about as big as her body. She fills the sac with 200 or 300 bright yellow eggs. Each one of the eggs will develop into a baby spider, or *spiderling*.

After all the eggs are laid, the black widow spins a silky covering for the sac and attaches it to her web. The black widow stays near the sac to protect her eggs from danger. This is not a good time to put your finger in her web!

A few weeks later, a hole appears in the egg sac and the spiderlings start to come out. The young spiders are clear and rubbery, with no markings. They swarm out of the egg sac and fill the web. The mother black widow watches her babies. If she is hungry, she will eat a few of them. The baby spiders are hungry, too, and they sometimes eat each other. When the black widow family has dinner together, it is dangerous for all concerned!

The spiderlings soon leave their mother's web. Some of them crawl off to the nearest dark corner and build their own web. But most of them find their way to the top of a plant, a fence post, or some other high place. They use their spinnerets to spin a long, light strand of silk. The air catches the silky strands and lifts them up into the air. This is called *ballooning*. The air currents carry them far away. When they land, they find a dark corner where they will build their first web.

The spiderlings grow quickly. Every week or two, the young spider gets too big for its hard, shell-like skin. It hangs from a strand of silk and flexes its body until its skin splits. Then it wriggles out of its old skin.

A black widow sheds its skin, or *molts*, several times before reaching its full size. The first time a black widow molts it is light gray or yellow with an orange abdomen. With each new skin the spider gets darker. When the female black widow molts for the final time, it becomes glossy black with a reddish orange hourglass on its belly.

Some people think that black widow spiders are fierce, bad-tempered, deadly poisonous creatures that should be killed on sight. The truth is, black widows are shy and secretive spiders that won't bite unless they are threatened. They help us by keeping the insect population under control, and they usually build their webs in out-of-the-way places. But that doesn't mean you should let a black widow live under your bed! These little spiders are dangerous. You don't want to mess with the black widow spider!

THE CHILD'S WORLD
NATUREBOOKS

Wildlife Library

Alligators	Musk-oxen
Arctic Foxes	Octopuses
Bald Eagles	Owls
Beavers	Penguins
Birds	Polar Bears
Black Widows	Primates
Camels	Rattlesnakes
Cheetahs	Reptiles
Coyotes	Rhinoceroses
Dogs	Seals and Sea Lions
Dolphins	Sharks
Elephants	Snakes
Fish	Spiders
Giraffes	Tigers
Insects	Walruses
Kangaroos	Whales
Lions	Wildcats
Mammals	Wolves
Monarchs	Zebras

Space Library

Earth	The Moon
Mars	The Sun

Adventure Library

Glacier National Park	Yellowstone National Park
The Grand Canyon	Yosemite